MY FIRST

# Thanksgiving
## BOOK

by Jane Belk Moncure
illustrated by Gwen Connelly

created by The Child's World

 CHILDRENS PRESS, CHICAGO

**Library of Congress Cataloging in Publication Data**

Moncure, Jane Belk.
  My first Thanksgiving book.

  Summary: Focuses on various Thanksgiving themes,
including the Pilgrims, Indians, corn, pumpkin pie,
turkey, and thankfulness.
  1. Children's poetry, American.   2. Thanksgiving
Day—Juvenile poetry.   [1. Thanksgiving Day—
Poetry.   2. American poetry]   I. Connelly, Gwen, ill.
II. Child's World (Firm)   III. Title.
PS3563.O517M9  1984              811'.54              84-9433
ISBN 0-516-02903-7

7 8 9 10 11 R 93 92 91

# MY FIRST THANKSGIVING BOOK

# The Mayflower

The Mayflower was
a sailing ship
blown by winds
across the sea
when long ago
a little band
of Pilgrims came
to this new land—
America.

# Pilgrims

The Pilgrims came to this new land
because they wanted to be free—
   free to worship God as they
     believed they should.
They came because they wanted to
   make laws that would be
     fair and good—
laws that would treat everyone
         the same.
That is why the Pilgrims came.

# Plymouth

The Pilgrims landed at a place
   called Plymouth.
They anchored the ship
   in a quiet bay.
There were no friends to greet them
       no farms to feed them.
Except for the ship, there was
   no place to stay.
So the men built
   a long, long shelter
for their first home—far away.

# First Winter

The first winter in Plymouth
    was bitter cold.
Both young and old were sick
    and scared.
They feared the Indians soon
    would come with bows and
    arrows . . . but instead,
two Indians came with
    corn and bread.
Squanto and Samoset came to help,
bringing food to eat and seeds to
    grow.
They were the Pilgrims' very
    best friends
that icy winter long ago.

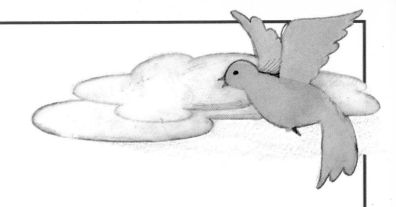

# Indian Ways

Squanto stayed with the Pilgrims
    for many days.
He taught the Pilgrims the Indian ways
    of hunting, fishing, and farming.
He taught them secrets the Indians knew.
Then the Pilgrims planted seeds—
        for squash and corn —
        pumpkins too!

# First Harvest

When the ears of corn were
    ripe in the field,
the Pilgrims gathered
    the golden grain.
It was time to give thanks
for the food they had grown
    in the summer sun
    and the autumn rain.

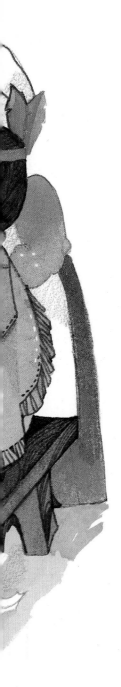

# Thanksgiving

"Let's give thanks," the Pilgrims said.
"Let's have a feast and invite our friends."
And so,
from deep in the forest
the Indians came — the chief and
ninety braves.
For three days they celebrated
the harvest,
eating together and
playing games
in peace and friendship.

# Popcorn

The Indians knew a secret
that the Pilgrims did not know
as they sat around the fire
a long time ago.
An Indian threw in some
corn — and then . . .
it popped and popped and
popped again.
Popcorn was a gift
of friendship from the Indians.

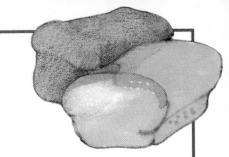

# A Family Time

Thanksgiving is that time of year
when people come from far and near.
The family grows from three or four
to five or six or ten or more.
The table may be large or small,
but room is made for one and all!

# Pumpkin Pies

The Indians gave the Pilgrims
a very nice surprise. . .
when they gave them pumpkins
   for spicy pumpkin pies.
After our Thanksgiving dinner,
when everyone is through,
I help Mom serve pumpkin pies.
I helped make them too.

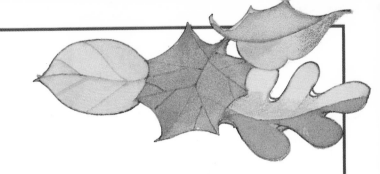

# Two Magic Words

Thanksgiving has two magic words.
To find them, try this stunt.
Just cut Thanksgiving right
    in two.
Now put the last word
    up in front.

# Sharing

I said to my mom, "Teacher wants
   us to fill a Thanksgiving basket."
Mom gave me a big pumpkin and some
   cranberry bread.
She helped me make a card that
   said,
      HAPPY THANKSGIVING!
Thanksgiving is fun to share. . .
   a special time to say,
      "We care."

# Colors

Pumpkin orange and roast turkey brown
are Thanksgiving colors all over town—
with corn pudding yellow,
    cranberry red,
        salad green,
            and golden bread.
Look out the window and you will see
Thanksgiving colors upon the trees.
I wonder how the trees are able
to have colors like a
        THANKSGIVING TABLE!

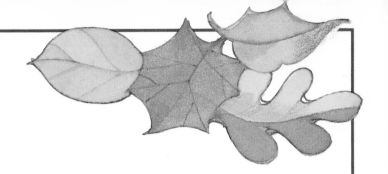

# Being Thankful

For all our food,
for what we wear,
for all the good things,
everywhere,
we're thankful.